Dreams by Day, Dreams by Night

An Anthology of Poems and Photographs

Foreword by

Nikki Grimes

Photograph Credits:
Cover: © Dale O'Dell/Corbis Stock Market; p. 1: © John Lund/Getty Images, Inc.; p. 7: © Marc Soloman/Getty Images, Inc.; p. 9: © Charles Settrington/Getty Images, Inc.; p. 11: © Steve Niedorf Photography/Getty Images, Inc.; p. 13: © Ralph H. Wetmore II/Desert Dolphin; p. 15: © Mike Howell/H. Armstrong Roberts, Inc.; p. 17: Brian Bailey/Getty Images, Inc.; p. 19: © Darryl Torckler/Getty Images, Inc.; p. 21: © David Paterson/Getty Images, Inc.; p. 23: © Lori Adamski Peek/Getty Images, Inc.; p. 25: © Christopher J. Boyle/Photonica; p. 27: © Jeremy Walker/Getty Images, Inc.; p. 29: © Zefa Zeitgeist/Photonica; p. 31: © 2002 Jay Corbett; p. 32: © Rich Kirchner/Photo Researchers, Inc.

For information contact:
MONDO Publishing
980 Avenue of the Americas
New York, NY 10018

Visit our website at www.mondopub.com

Printed in China

02 03 04 05 06 07   HC   9 8 7 6 5 4 3 2 1
   09 10 11 12   PB   9 8 7 6 5 4 3 2

ISBN 1-59034-390-5   1-59034-479-0 (pbk)
Designed by Symon Chow

Library of Congress Cataloging-in-Publication Data

Dreams by day, dreams by night : an anthology of poems and photographs / foreword by Nikki Grimes.
        p. cm.
     Summary: Poems and photographs present all sorts of dreams--daydreams, nighttime dreams, hopes and aspirations.
     ISBN 1-59034-390-5 (hc) -- ISBN 1-59034-479-0 (pbk)
     1. Dreams--Juvenile poetry. 2. Children's poetry, American. [1. Dreams--Poetry. 2. American poetry--Collections.]

  811.008'0353--dc 21

                    2002074339

Every effort has been made to trace the ownership of all copyright materials in this book and to obtain permission for their use. Grateful acknowledgment is made to the following for permission to reprint copyright materials:

"Dreams" by Langston Hughes. From THE COLLECTED POEMS OF LANGSTON HUGHES by Langston Hughes, copyright © 1994 by The Estate of Langston Hughes. Used by permission of Alfred A. Knopf, a division of Random House, Inc.

"Nighttime" by Lee Bennett Hopkins. Copyright © 2000 by Lee Bennett Hopkins. First appeared in GOOD RHYMES, GOOD TIMES, published by HarperCollins Publishers. Reprinted by permission of Curtis Brown, Ltd.

"If I Were in Charge of the World" by Judith Viorst. Reprinted with the permission of Atheneum Books for Young Readers, an imprint of Simon & Schuster Children's Publishing Division from IF I WERE IN CHARGE OF THE WORLD AND OTHER WORRIES by Judith Viorst. Text copyright © 1981 Judith Viorst.

"Waking Up" by Siv Cedering. Copyright © Siv Cedering, THE BLUE HORSE, Clarion Books, 1979.

"Statue of Liberty" by Myra Cohn Livingston. Reprinted with the permission of Margaret K. McElderry Books, an imprint of Simon & Schuster Children's Publishing Division from I NEVER TOLD AND OTHER POEMS by Myra Cohn Livingston. Text copyright © 1992 Myra Cohn Livingston.

"Frozen Dream" by Shel Silverstein. Copyright © 1981 by Evil Eye Music, Inc. Used by permission of HarperCollins Publishers.

"I Dream a Dream" by Felice Holman. Permission of the author. From THE SONG IN MY HEAD by Felice Holman. Copyright © 1985 Charles Scribner's Sons.

"The Winter Tree" by Douglas Florian. Copyright © 1999 by Douglas Florian. Used by permission of HarperCollins Publishers.

"Running Shoes" by Nikki Grimes. From SHOE MAGIC by Nikki Grimes. Published by Orchard Books, an imprint of Scholastic Inc. Copyright © 2000 by Nikki Grimes. Reprinted by permission.

"Waking Up" by Eleanor Farjeon. Reprinted with the permission of Macmillan from BLACKBIRD HAS SPOKEN by Eleanor Farjeon. Copyright © Eleanor Farjeon.

"School Day" by Charlotte Zolotow. Copyright © 1967, copyright © renewed 1995 by Charlotte Zolotow. Reprinted by permission of S©ott Treimel NY.

"The Butterfly Jar," from THE BUTTERFLY JAR by Jeff Moss, copyright © 1989 by Jeff Moss. Used by permission of Bantam Books, a division of Random House, Inc.

"Dream Maker" by Jane Yolen. Copyright © 1993 by Jane Yolen. First appeared in WHAT RHYMES WITH MOON?, published by Philomel, a Division of Penguin Putnam, Inc. Reprinted by permission of Curtis Brown, Ltd.

Contents

Foreword

"Hold fast to dreams" wrote Langston Hughes, "For if dreams die/Life is a broken-winged bird/That cannot fly." But what exactly is a dream? A wish? A hope? A fantasy? Dreams are all those things. And whether they press against the panes of classroom windows as we stare out, or creep into our heads while we sleep, it's difficult to overestimate their power.

Dreams drive us to try things we never have, travel to places we've never been, climb heights we thought we'd never dare. A dream is a ticket to ride from our imaginings out into the real world—a world full of possibility.

What are your dreams? Here, poets like Jane Yolen and Langston Hughes tell us what they think of dreams. Lee Bennett Hopkins and Siv Cedering write about the wonder of dreams. Others of us share day dreams and night *dreams, dreams of flying, and dreams of running. Here, a statue dreams, and so does a tree. Shel Silverstein even shares a frozen dream!*

Enjoy this book and when you're done, take a cue from us. Dream. Dream of who you'll become and where you'll go. Dream of the canvas of the world and what it would look like if the paintbrush were in your hand. Dream as you muse into the sun or doze under the moon. Any time of day will do!

There are millions of dreams and just as many definitions. For me, a dream is a seed you plant in the garden of your heart. It's spindly at first, but if you water it with care, give it light and love, and protect it from the cold, one fine day it will bloom, bright and beautiful—and yours!

—Nikki Grimes

Dreams

Hold fast to dreams
For if dreams die
Life is a broken-winged bird
That cannot fly.

Hold fast to dreams
For when dreams go
Life is a barren field
Frozen with snow.

Langston Hughes

Marc Solomon

Nighttime

How do dreams know

when to creep

Into my head

when I fall off

to sleep?

Lee Bennett Hopkins

Charles Settrington

If I Were in Charge of the World

If I were in charge of the world
I'd cancel oatmeal,
Monday mornings,
Allergy shots, and also Sara Steinberg.

If I were in charge of the world
There'd be brighter night-lights,
Healthier hamsters, and
Basketball baskets forty-eight inches lower.

If I were in charge of the world
You wouldn't have lonely.
You wouldn't have clean.
You wouldn't have bedtimes.
Or "Don't punch your sister."
You wouldn't even have sisters.

If I were in charge of the world
A chocolate sundae with whipped cream and nuts would be a vegetable,
All 007 movies would be G,
And a person who sometimes forgot to brush,
And sometimes forgot to flush,
Would still be allowed to be
In charge of the world.

Judith Viorst

Steve Niedorf Photography

10

Waking Up

What?

    Oh.

        Where am I?

I thought I could fly.

            I did.

I did fly.

       The sky

was my road,

        and I was floating,

                swooping,

sweeping the air

        with a pair

of wings

      like a hawk

        or swallow.

And then

      I woke up

        here on my pillow.

So I guess

     I was just

       sleeping.

Siv Cedering

Ralph H. Wetmore II

Statue of Liberty

Give me your tired, your poor, she says,

Those yearning to be free.

Take a light from my burning torch,

The light of liberty.

Give me your huddled masses

Lost on another shore,

Tempest-tossed and weary,

These I will take and more.

Give me your thirsty, your hungry

Who come from another place.

You who would dream of freedom

Look into my face.

Myra Cohn Livingston

Mike Howell

Frozen Dream

I'll take the dream I had last night
And put it in my freezer,
So someday long and far away
When I'm an old grey geezer,
I'll take it out and thaw it out,
This lovely dream I've frozen,
And boil it up and sit me down
And dip my old cold toes in.

Shel Silverstein

Brian Bailey

I Dream a Dream

I dream a dream by day

a wish, a hope

a fitful fantasy

in which what isn't *is*,

and where what is

has changed

or gone away.

I dream a dream by night

a distant trek

a journey through moonlight,

and then what was seems dear,

and waking finds that all that is

is right.

Felice Holman

Darryl Torckler

The Winter Tree

The winter tree

Is fast asleep.

She dreams, in reams

Of snow knee-deep,

Of children climbing

Up her trunk,

Of white-tailed deer

And gray chipmunk,

Of picnics,

Hammocks,

And short sleeves,

And leaves

And leaves

And leaves

And leaves.

Douglas Florian

David Paterson

Running Shoes

Olympic dreams

Sing me to sleep at night,

And the very sight

Of fancy running shoes

Gets me thinking:

Man! With shoes like those

I wouldn't run—I'd fly.

But my poor pockets

Are only lined with lint.

I could take the hint,

Give up my dreaming.

But words from Daddy

Once whispered in secret

Send my doubts

Into hasty retreat:

"It's not the shoes

That do the runnin'.

It's the feet."

Nikki Grimes

Lori Adamski Peek

Waking Up

Oh! I have just had such a lovely dream!

And then I woke,

And all the dream went out like kettle-steam,

Or chimney-smoke.

      My dream was all about — how funny, though!

            I've only just

      Dreamed it, and now it has begun to blow

            Away like dust.

In it I went — no! In my dream I had—

No, that's not it!

I can't remember, oh, it is too bad,

My dream a bit.

      But I saw something beautiful, I'm sure—

            Then someone spoke,

      And then I didn't see it anymore,

            Because I woke.

Eleanor Farjeon

Christopher J. Boyle

The Land of Nod

From breakfast on through all the day
At home among my friends I stay,
But every night I go abroad
Afar into the land of Nod.

All by myself I have to go,
With none to tell me what to do—
All alone beside the streams
And up the mountain–sides of dreams.

The strangest things are there for me,
Both things to eat and things to see,
And many frightening sights abroad
Till morning in the land of Nod.

Try as I like to find the way,
I never can get back by day,
Nor can remember plain and clear
The curious music that I hear.

Robert Louis Stevenson

Jeremy Walker

School Day

I don't mean to look

but I can't help seeing

a bit of sky outside the schoolhouse window.

I don't mean to watch

but I can't help watching

the maple branch that brushes against the pane.

I don't mean to dream

but I can't help dreaming

that I could be wandering

under the sky,

        watching the leaves

        watching the trees

        as the wind goes by.

Charlotte Zolotow

Zefa Zeitgeist

The Butterfly Jar

We had a jar with a butterfly.

We opened the lid and it flew to the sky.

And there are things inside my head

Waiting to be thought or said,

Dreams and jokes and wonderings are

Locked inside, like a butterfly jar.

But then, when you are here with me,

I can open the lid and set them free.

Jeff Moss

Jay Corbett

Dream Maker

The shining silver moon
Is a coin hung in the sky
To pay the old Dream Maker
Whenever he goes by.

Jane Yolen

Rich Kirchner